T0287410

LONDON'S
LOW-FLOOR BUSES

LONDON'S LOW-FLOOR BUSES

DAVID BEDDALL

AMBERLEY

Acknowledgements

First and foremost, I would like to sincerely thank Liam Farrer-Beddall for always supporting me in my projects for Amberley; for allowing me access to his vast collection of London bus photographs, and for taking the time to read through my drafts. I would also like to thank Ian Armstrong for again allowing me to use some of his photographs to fill in gaps.

First published 2020

Amberley Publishing
The Hill, Stroud
Gloucestershire, GL5 4EP

www.amberley-books.com

Copyright © David Beddall, 2020

The right of David Beddall to be identified as the Authors of this work has been asserted in accordance with the Copyright, Designs and Patents Act 1988.

ISBN 978 1 3981 0119 7 (print)
ISBN 978 1 3981 0120 3 (ebook)

All rights reserved. No part of this book may be reprinted or reproduced or utilised in any form or by any electronic, mechanical or other means, now known or hereafter invented, including photocopying and recording, or in any information storage or retrieval system, without the permission in writing from the Publishers.

British Library Cataloguing in Publication Data. A catalogue record for this book is available from the British Library.

Origination by Amberley Publishing.
Printed in the UK.

Introduction

The low-floor bus was first introduced to London at the end of December 1993 when the first Wright Pathfinder-bodied Dennis Lance SLF saloons arrived with London United, entering service in 1994. These were followed by a batch of Scania L113CRL with similar bodywork. Operating on four routes, no further orders for this type were placed.

The first significant orders for low-floor buses was placed in 1996 when the Dennis Dart SLF model was introduced. This became the most popular low-floor single-decker to operate in London between 1996 and 2006. Bodywork on the type was available from Plaxton, Alexander, East Lancs and Marshalls.

1997 saw the arrival of the first low-floor double-deckers, with the appearance of the Alexander ALX400 and Plaxton President. DAF produced the first chassis, with the DB250LF model, just beating Dennis, who introduced the new Trident. It wasn't until 1999 that Volvo offered an alternative to these – the B7TL. The privatised operators favoured certain models over others, and this will be seen in this book. Another popular choice was the Wrightbus Eclipse Gemini, which was introduced in 2001.

Other manufacturers offered low-floor models, but these were not as popular as those mentioned above. DAF offered the SB120 saloon, Mercedes-Benz the Citaro and Citaro G. Scania offered the N94UD and N230UD double-decks, the latter model becoming popular with several operators.

The second generation of low-floor buses were introduced in 2006 – the Enviro 200 and 400 models produced by Alexander Dennis Limited (ADL). These two new types replaced the ALX200, ALX400 and Plaxton President. As with the first generation, Wrightbus was late in producing an updated version of the Gemini – the Gemini 2 – which became available from 2009. Despite the late arrival, this latter model became popular with London operators.

A third generation arrived in the mid-2010s, with Wrightbus introducing the Streetdeck and Gemini 3 models; while ADL introduced the MMC (Major Model Change) range, along with the new Enviro 400 City model, which took aspects from the New Bus for London.

The Wrightbus New Bus for London (NBfL) itself was introduced to London service in 2012, with the first full route conversion taking place in 2013. This was the first bus to be produced specifically for London since the AEC Routemaster in 1954. By the time production ceased in 2018, 1,000 of these vehicles had been built. A similar model, known as the SRM, was built on the Volvo B5LH chassis, but only a handful were made.

A newcomer to the London scene was MCV, who introduced the EvoSeti model in 2015. MCV had introduced another double-deck body in 2011, but this was not as popular as the EvoSeti. MCV also produced the Evolution single-deck body, which had been taken into stock in small numbers by Metroline and Metrobus. Go-Ahead London, Metroline and Tower Transit took sizable orders of the EvoSeti.

Since 2003, London has been involved in a number of trials of various types of bus, some of which ran on alternative fuel to diesel. The first such vehicles arrived running on hydrogen fuel cells. Two further types have also been trialled using this technology over the years. The first significant step towards introducing all-electric buses commenced in 2015 when the first all-electric vehicles were introduced, with three ADL Enviro 400 MMCs entering service with Tower Transit. These were followed by five BYD double-decks with Metroline. BYD has become one of the leading manufacturers in producing all-electric buses, with a growing number of vehicles being introduced. The single-deck model is becoming popular on central London routes. Metroline introduced the first production batch of BYD double-decks to route 43.

The aim of this book is to offer a potted history of the low-floor bus between 1993 and December 2019.

Wrightbus of Ballymena was the first to offer a low-floor body with the Pathfinder model on both the Scania and Dennis chassis. Thirty-eight Dennis Lance SLF saloons were delivered to London Buses in 1993 and 1994. The first ten arrived with London United in December 1993 for the take up of route 120 (Hounslow Bus Station–Northolt Station) in January 1994. LLW9 (ODZ 8909) was one of the ten vehicles for the 120. It is seen off route operating the H37, showing off the low-floor branding applied to these early vehicles. (Ian Armstrong Collection)

Centrewest took stock of the next fourteen Dennis Lance SLFs at Uxbridge garage. They were taken into stock to operate route 222 (Uxbridge Station–Hounslow Bus Station). The low-floor branding can be seen again on LLW24 (ODZ 8924), which is seen exiting Uxbridge Station bound for Hounslow. Metroline took stock of the remaining fourteen LLWs for route 186 (Brent Cross–Northwick Park Hospital). (Ian Armstrong Collection)

Ordered alongside the Dennis Lance SLFs were thirty Wright Pathfinder-bodied Scania N113CRLs. The first fifteen were delivered to Leaside Buses just before privatisation, passing to their new owner in 1994. Like the Lance SLFs, branding was applied to these vehicles to show off the low-floor design. The route chosen for these vehicles was the 144 (Muswell Hill–Edmonton Green), on which route SLW12 (RDZ 1712) is seen showing off the branding applied. (Ian Armstrong Collection)

The second half of the thirty Scanias went to East London, which became Stagecoach London in September 1994. They were put to use on route 101 (North Woolwich Ferry–Manor House). The initial livery was the same as shown on SLW12, but in 2001 Stagecoach introduced a new livery for its UK bus operations. The London version is seen applied to SLW26 (RDZ 6126) along with the new logos. (Ian Armstrong Collection)

Plaxton was the first to offer a low-floor body style on the Dennis Dart SLF saloon, with a revised version of the popular Pointer model. The demonstrator went to Centrewest, while Go-Ahead London took the first production models in November 1996, just slightly after the ALX200 model. The Plaxton Pointer became the most popular body style to be placed on the Dart SLF chassis, with many London operators taking stock of the type until it was replaced by the Enviro200 in 2006. LDP9 (P509 RYM) is seen on layover at Sutton garage. (David Beddall)

London United purchased a large number of Pointer Darts up until 2006. One of the first to be purchased is seen on layover at Hounslow Bus Station. DP13 (T413 KAG) was originally taken into stock by the company to operate a route between Heathrow and Feltham rail station. After this service finished, the vehicles were placed into normal service with the company. (Liam Farrer-Beddall)

Harrow finds DPS639 (SK02 XHP), one of fifty-seven Pointer Darts taken into stock by London United during 2002 for general fleet replacement. Some were later transferred to London Sovereign to replace similar, older V-plate Dart SLF saloons on Harrow area local services. (Liam Farrer-Beddall)

Stagecoach East London took stock of the first Alexander ALX200-bodied Dennis Dart SLF saloons in London in April 1996, just after the arrival of the Plaxton Pointer model that went on demonstration to Centrewest. This was to become one of the more popular body styles to be fitted to the Dart SLF chassis. The majority worked with Stagecoach, with Epsom Buses and Armchair taking stock of small batches of the type. SLD7 (P27 HMF) was one of the first ALX200s to arrive in London. (Ian Armstrong Collection)

Another view of the ALX200 body style is seen here while operating service 100. SLD57 (R457 FVX), later 34057 with Stagecoach, is seen at Liverpool Street Bus Station, operating from Stratford garage. The Dennis and Alexander badges can be clearly seen on the bumper of this vehicle. (Ian Armstrong Collection)

London United's first choice for the Dennis Dart SLF body was the Wright Crusader model. Taking up service in October 1996 on the H25 (Hanworth–Hatton Cross Station), these vehicles were built to single-door layout. November 2001 saw the loss of the H25 to Tellings Golden Miller, seeing the Darts transfer to other garages within London United. They were all reunited in May 2002 at Stamford Brook where they took up service on new route 440 (Stamford Brook Garage–Park Royal Asda). They remained on this service until 2006 when they moved on to Yellow Buses. In March 2003 the 440 was extended to Stonebridge Park, and it is this destination we see CD2 (VDZ 8002) heading towards. (Ian Armstrong Collection)

Metrobus brought a splash of colour to the London scene with its distinctive blue and yellow livery. The 358 (Orpington–Bromley–Crystal Palace) had become a successful route for the company, with patronage outgrowing the capacity of the original vehicles purchased for the route. To combat this, ten Optare Excels were purchased in August 1996 – the first of their type in London. Operating from Green Street Green garage, P503 OUG is seen here representing the batch bound for Orpington Station. (Ian Armstrong Collection)

Six Optare Excel saloons were taken into stock by Westlink to replace a similar number of Optare Vectra-bodied MAN saloons in June 1997. They were initially put to use on route 371 (Richmond–Kingston) and were given route branding. The introduction of new Dennis Dart SLF saloons in 2000 saw the Excels move to Hounslow, mainly for use on the 110 (Twickenham–Hounslow). It is on this route we find XL1 (P151 BUG). (Ian Armstrong Collection)

National Express entered the London market as Travel London, winning the contracts for routes C11 and 211 in 1998. The 211 (Waterloo Station–Hammersmith Bus Station) saw twenty-one Optare Excels taken into stock. Hammersmith Bus Station finds R415 HWU, displaying the smart livery worn by Travel London buses. (Ian Armstrong Collection)

Alexander developed the first low-floor double-deck bus body, which was released in 1998. Known as the ALX400, this type became the most popular low-floor double-deck in London service. DAF just beat Dennis to introducing the first low-floor double-decker, the DB250 model. The only customer for the type in London was the Arriva Group. DLA34 (S234 JUA) is seen while operating rail replacement duties at Walthamstow Central. (David Beddall)

Waterloo finds another fine example of the DAF DB250/Alexander ALX400 combination. DLA279 (Y479 UGC) is seen blinded for its return journey to Wood Green. The revised Arriva London livery of red, with a yellow band can be seen in this view. (Liam Farrer-Beddall)

2003 saw the last of the DLA-class delivered to Arriva London, before the type bowed out to the Wright Eclipse Pulsar model on the same chassis. Showing the 100 per cent red livery that was implemented on all London buses is DLA380 (LJ03 MTY), parked on the forecourt of Thornton Heath garage. (Liam Farrer-Beddall)

Dennis developed the Trident model at the same time as DAF, with the Trident becoming the more popular choice among London operators. Stagecoach London took delivery of over 1,000 Trident/ALX400s, taking the first and last examples of the type into stock. Romford Station finds 17114 (V114 MEV) showing off the smart body style of this type. (Liam Farrer-Beddall)

Metroline was another customer for the Alexander ALX400/Dennis Trident combination. The company took stock of fifty-two of these vehicles during 1999. Representing this batch is TA73 (T43 KLD), seen about to enter Edgware Bus Station having just completed a journey on route 32. It is seen wearing the distinctive blue skirt worn by Metroline's fleet during the 1990s and 2000s. (Liam Farrer-Beddall)

London United also favoured the Alexander ALX400-bodied Dennis Trident model, taking 156 of these vehicles between 2000 and 2003. TA317 (SN03 DZS) was one of thirty-five ALX400s delivered to the company in 2003. It is seen passing through Kingston, bound for Tooting Broadway on route 131. (Liam Farrer-Beddall)

Centrewest London and its successor First London took stock of a large quantity of the Marshall Capital-bodied Dennis Dart SLF saloon from its introduction to London in 1997, until the demise of Marshall in 2003. DML41387 (X387 HLR) shows off the type well while parked at Hayes garage. (Liam Farrer-Beddall)

Another view of the Marshall Capital body style is seen here at Golders Green, where we find DM41449 (LN51 DUY). Although First London took stock of the largest amount of this type, they were not the only ones to do so. Go-Ahead London and Metroline also took smaller quantities of the type into stock. (Liam Farrer-Beddall)

The East Lancs Spryte bodywork proved to be an unpopular model with London operators. Thirteen were taken into stock by Capital Citybus during January and February 1998, with seven others being purchased by Wings for operation in north-west London. 713 (R713 VLA) is seen here on layover at Stratford Bus Station in the distinctive yellow livery worn by Capital Citybus. (Ian Armstrong Collection)

The first Optare Solos entered service in London during 1998 with the original Travel London operation. The red livery was relieved by a white and blue stripe, as can be seen above. Representing the batch is S231 EWU. (Ian Armstrong Collection)

First Essex introduced the Optare Solo midibus to the Romford area in March 2002 when eleven such vehicles were put to use on the 193 (Romford Oldchurch Hospital–County Park Estate). 501 (EO02 FLA) is seen wearing the First London style livery applied to these vehicles. Romford Station provides the location of this photograph. (David Beddall)

Epsom Buses/Quality Line were the biggest operator of the Optare Solo model in London with over forty of the standard and SR model being operated. OP14 (YN53 SUF) was new to the company in September 2003. It is seen heading for Colliers Wood Station, passing through Sutton town centre. (Liam Farrer-Beddall)

Over the years, Walthamstow became an area which saw several Solo routes operate. First London introduced the type to the area in 2005 with a small batch of six on route W12 (Walthamstow–Wanstead). 53704 (LK05 DXS) is seen exiting Walthamstow Bus Station for the short journey to Coppermill Lane. (David Beddall)

Metroline took up operation of route 346 in Watford in 2005 using five Optare Solos. Representing the batch is NSM660 (YK05 CCD), seen in the infamous Metroline livery. Watford town centre provides the location of this photograph. (David Beddall)

Golders Green is the central location on routes H2 and H3 serving the Hampstead Garden Village area, the H3 extending out to East Finchley. Arriva The Shires took stock of five Solos in June 2006 for the two routes, being allocated to Garston garage. OS69 (YJ06 YRR) was originally numbered 2469 and is seen in between duties at Golders Green. (Liam Farrer-Beddall)

March 2010 saw the W12 pass to CT plus, who also operated Optare Solos on the route. OS6 (YJ10 EYH) is seen about to enter Walthamstow Bus Station. (Liam Farrer-Beddall)

Metroline took stock of the first Plaxton Presidents in London service, these being on the Dennis Trident chassis, beating the DAF DB250 by a few months. TP22 (T122 KLD) is seen starting its journey at Archway, bound for Waterloo. (Liam Farrer-Beddall)

First London also took stock of a large number of the Plaxton President-bodied Dennis Trident. A sizeable batch was allocated to Greenford garage where they were put to use on routes into both Greenford and Ealing. TN32993 (Y993 NLP) is captured at Ealing Broadway before heading back to Greenford on route E1. (Liam Farrer-Beddall)

A more modest fifty Trident/President vehicles were taken into stock by Go-Ahead London, all allocated to Stockwell garage. PDL28 (PN03 ULK) is seen on layover at Victoria while operating a rail replacement service. (David Beddall)

Shortly after the Plaxton President-bodied Dennis Tridents arrived with Metroline, Arriva London took stock of the President-bodied DAF DB250 model. Enfield finds two of the type, DLP18 and DLP48. DLP18 (T218 XBV) is the one nearest the camera and was delivered to Arriva London North in October 1999. (David Beddall)

Another view of the parking ground in Enfield. This time, DLP66 (LJ51 DKY) poses for the camera before setting off for Turnpike Lane Station on route 329. Capital Logistics was the only other operator in London to take stock of the DAF DB250/ Plaxton President combination. (David Beddall)

September 1999 saw independent London Traveller gain the contracts for routes 187 (Queens Park–Central Middlesex Hospital) and 487 (Willesden Junction–South Harrow Station). For these two routes, fifteen East Lancs Spryte-bodied Volvo B6BLE saloons were purchased. V508 EFR shows the original livery, the red being relieved by yellow stripes. (Ian Armstrong Collection)

July 1999 saw the arrival of another body style on the Dennis Trident chassis. Metrobus ordered fifteen East Lancs Loylne-bodied Tridents for the take up of route 161 (Chislehurst–North Greenwich). 411 (T411 EMV) is seen paused at Eltham Station. Overall, twenty-eight vehicles of this combination were taken into stock by the company, with twenty-three further examples being purchased by Blue Triangle. (Ian Armstrong Collection)

Seventeen East Lancs Myllennium-bodied DAF SB220 saloons were taken into stock by London Central in 1999 for use on routes M1 and M2, centred on the Millennium Dome at North Greenwich. For this, special registrations were given to these vehicles ending in GMT. Once the Dome closed at the end of 2000, they moved from New Cross to Bexleyheath where they were used on the 486 between Bexleyheath and North Greenwich Station. Showing this smart bodywork is MD10 (V10 GMT). (Ian Armstrong Collection)

The President-bodied Volvo B7TL was the last of the three chassis types to enter service carrying the ALX400 body. London Central was the first to take stock of the type in December 1999, entering service in early 2000 from Peckham. London United was next to take the type into stock. VA76 (V192 OOE) represents the Volvo B7TL/ALX400 combination, seen at rest at Hounslow garage. First London and Arriva London also took delivery of the type. (Liam Farrer-Beddall)

President-bodied Volvo B7TL became one of the popular first generation low-floor buses with a number of operators taking stock of the type. Go-Ahead London took over 400 of the type between 2000 and 2004. The first thirty-eight 'PVL' class arrived during March and April 2000 and were allocated to Bexleyheath. PVL16 (V816 KGF) is seen about to enter Bexleyheath town centre, carrying London Central fleet names. (Liam Farrer-Beddall)

Metroline was another big customer of the Plaxton President-bodied Volvo B7TL, taking two different lengths into stock. The longer version was classified VPL and is represented by VPL183 (Y183 NLK) seen departing Victoria for Willesden bus garage. Willesden was home to a large number of Volvo B7TLs of both lengths. (David Beddall)

Another Go-Ahead London Volvo B7TL is seen in this view passing through Lewisham, heading towards Foots Cray Tesco. New Cross-based PVL347 (PF52 WPX) is the vehicle concerned. To the left of the picture, an Alexander ALX400-bodied Dennis Trident can be seen, this being the main competition to the President. The more subtle London Central fleet names can be seen on the vehicle. (Liam Farrer-Beddall)

First London also operated examples of the B7TL/President combination. VNL32306 (LK03 NHF) was new to the company in May 2003 as VTL1306, being renumbered into the five-digit series in October of the same year. It was allocated to Northumberland Park garage where it operated route 67. First sold this garage to Go-Ahead London in March 2012, with VNL32306 becoming PVN1 in that fleet. It is seen on layover in Wood Green. (David Beddall)

An impressive eighty-six B7TL/Presidents were taken into stock at Willesden garage, primarily for routes 6 and 98. VP503 (LK53 LXW) is seen passing out of service through Marble Arch, heading back to Willesden. It is seen wearing the 100 per cent red livery. (Liam Farrer-Beddall)

The Caetano Nimbus-bodied Dart SLF saloon had been taken into stock by Hackney Community Transport, Mitcham Belle and Metrobus in small numbers prior to 2003. The type gained a significant order from First London in 2003 following the collapse of Marshalls of Cambridge. Fifty-three such vehicles were taken into stock over the course of 2003 by First. Representing the sizeable batch is DMC41514 (LK03 NGG), which is seen passing Romford Station. The smart First London livery can be seen here. (Liam Farrer-Beddall)

The first Wright Cadet-bodied DAF SB120 saloon entered service with Arriva London in August 2000 from Wood Green. Just over a year passed before the first production models arrived in the capital. Arriva London took stock of an intial batch of twenty-two such saloons at Brixton for route 319. They remained on this route until September 2006 when they were reallocated with the company. The forecourt of Thornton Heath garage finds DWL2 (Y802 DGT), its third allocation within the company. (David Beddall)

While under the control of Arriva The Shires, Arriva East Herts & Essex purchased fourteen DAF SB120 saloons for routes 256 (Noak Hill–Hornchurch Hospital) and 346 (Upminister Station–Upminister Park Estate), allocated to Grays. Delivery commenced in November 2001, and two months later control passed to Arriva Southern Counties, and so did the vehicles. Originally operated in the turquoise and cream livery, they were repainted into the standard red livery. 3501 (KE51 PTZ) is seen off route at Lakeside, operating route 370 from Romford. (Liam Farrer-Beddall)

The autumn of 2002 saw a large batch of DAF SB120 saloons arrive at Arriva London North's Wood Green garage, where they were used on routes 184 (Barnet Church–Turnpike Lane Station) and 298 (Potters Bar–Arnos Grove). Twelve of this batch were converted to driver training vehicles after a change in the rules relating to such vehicles. DWL32 (LF02 PNE) is seen parked at Ponders End garage wearing the white and grey training livery. (David Beddall)

East Thames Buses was the only other London operator to take stock of the SB120 model from new, with these passing to Go-Ahead London. Twelve shorter SB120s arrived in 2003 to take up route on the 393 (Clapton–Holloway). After the loss of the route, the vehicles were reallocated to Ash Grove, and then under the control of Go-Ahead London moved about even more. DW12 LF52 ZKA is seen parked at North Greenwich Station with its new owner on route 132. (Liam Farrer-Beddall)

Eighteen shorter Wright Cadet-bodied VDL SB120 saloons were introduced to route 410 (Wallington–Crystal Palace) when the longer 10 m DWL-class were deemed unsuitable for the route. The DWS classification code was given to these vehicles. Croydon finds DWS3 (LJ53 NHB) heading to West Croydon before continuing onto Wallington. (Liam Farrer-Beddall)

Wrightbus of Ballymena constructed its first double-deck body in 2001, with it being well received by operators, not only in London, but around the UK. Arriva London took a large quantity of the type, along with several other operators. East Thames Buses took stock of the type in 2002 when forty-four were purchased. When the company was acquired by Go-Ahead London in September 2009, these were added to the 273 similar vehicles already in stock with Go-Ahead, classified 'WVL'. To avoid confusion, the East Thames examples retained the VWL class code allotted to them by their former owner. VWL16 (LF52 TGN) represents the 317-strong batch operated by the Go-Ahead London group after 2009. It is seen passing through Eltham town centre. (Liam Farrer-Beddall)

WVL36 (LF52 ZRU) represents the large batch of 273 Wright Eclipse Gemini-bodied Volvo B7TLs taken into stock by Go-Ahead London, mentioned above. WVL36 is seen passing through Marble Arch, while operating from Putney garage. (Liam Farrer-Beddall)

The Eclipse Gemini was the first double-deck body built by Wrightbus and was first introduced to the London market in 2001, and by no stretch of the imagination became a big success. Arriva London took stock of the first examples of the type on the Volvo B7TL. First London and Go-Ahead London were also fans of the type, taking a large quantity of the type into stock between 2002 and 2006. First London's VNZ32343 (LK53 LZD) represents the type, passing Wembley Stadium on route 92. (Liam Farrer-Beddall)

Wright Eclipse Gemini-bodied Volvo B7TL LK55 ACU was new to First London as VNW32658. It is seen with new owner Metroline, who took over part of the First London operation in June 2013. Numbered VW1560 with its new owner, it is seen having just left Uxbridge garage to start a journey on the 'express' service 607 to White City. (Liam Farrer-Beddall)

Six Volvo articulated buses were placed into service with First London in October 2001 on trunk route 207 (Hayes Bypass–Shepherds Bush). Two of these were Wright Eclipse Fusion-bodied Volvo B7LAs acquired from First Southampton. AV2 (Y152 ROT) is seen above heading to Shepherds Bush. (Ian Armstrong Collection)

The remaining four articulated buses to be trialled on the 207 were Wright Fusion-bodied Volvo B10LAs acquired from First Glasgow. AV7 (V607 GGB) shows off the 'Barbie' livery worn by First buses in the provinces. (Ian Armstrong Collection)

First Capital took over the contract for the original route 395 (Limehouse–Surrey Quays) from Stagecoach London in 2002. For the route, a trio of Koch-bodied Mercedes-Benz Sprinter minibuses were taken into stock in March 2002. The last of these, ES799 (LT02 NVD), demonstrates the type. The 395 ran through the Rotherhithe Tunnel. (Ian Armstrong Collection)

The RV1 was a new route introduced in 2002 to make it easier for tourists to get between attractions located on the banks of the River Thames between the Tower of London and Covent Garden. For this, eleven Mercedes-Benz Citaro saloons were taken into stock by First Capital, allocated to their Hackney garage. ES64002 (originally EC2002) is seen on layover at the Covent Garden terminus. These vehicles carried Riverside branding, which can be seen on the side. (David Beddall)

Epsom Buses, trading as Quality Line, took stock of the next batch of Citaros in London service. Seven such vehicles were taken into stock in July 2003 for use on route 293 (Morden–Epsom Hospital), for which they carried appropriate route branding. The batch left the route in November 2008, with all but the first example going on long-term loan to Metrobus. MCL1 (BW03 ZMZ) is seen here attending the annual spring Cobham bus rally, at the Wisley Airfield. (Liam Farrer-Beddall)

London trialled a number of different alternative fuel buses, with RV1 being the selected route for these trials. The first were a trio of fuel cell-powered Mercedes-Benz Citaro saloons which arrived in December 2003. They remained operating alongside the traditional Citaros until their withdrawal in January 2007. Covent Garden is again the location of this photograph of ESQ64991 (LK53 MBO), seen advertising the fuel cell technology. (Liam Farrer-Beddall)

Fifty Citaro saloons were taken into stock by London General and allocated to Waterloo garage, where they displaced the thirty-one Citaro G bendy buses used on the two Red Arrow routes 507 and 521. Entry into service was complete by the end of August 2009. MEC8 (BG09 JKE) represents this large batch, waiting time at Waterloo Station. (Liam Farrer-Beddall)

Over the course of 2011 and 2012, the RATP group took seventeen Mercedes-Benz Citaro saloons into stock for its London United and Epsom Buses operations. The first seven were allocated to London United at Hounslow garage, from where they operated the 203 between Hounslow and Staines. MCL2 BD11 LWO is seen having just departed Hounslow Bus Station for Staines. The Epsom Buses batch were put to use on the X26 between West Croydon and Heathrow Airport. (Liam Farrer-Beddall)

Stagecoach London took stock of thirteen Mercedes-Benz Citaro saloons in May 2012 for route 227 (Bromley North–Crystal Palace). 23113 (LX12 DLN) represents the batch, allocated to Bromley garage, and is seen about to enter the Crystal Palace parking ground. The infamous transmitter dominates the skyline on the right of the photograph. (Liam Farrer-Beddall)

Nineteen of the modified Citaro saloons was taken into stock by Metrobus at Green Street Green garage in September 2015 to convert route 358 (Orpington Station–Crystal Palace) to the type. A fire at the Green Street Green garage destroyed three of these vehicles in November 2018. MEC64 (BF65 HVG) is seen passing through Bromley South bound for Crystal Palace. (Liam Farrer-Beddall)

The Red Arrow network were the first routes to gain the Mercedes-Benz Citaro G bendy-bus in London. Thirty-one were taken into stock by London General at Waterloo garage. The first, MAL1 (BX02 YZE), is seen in between duties parked at the Waterloo terminus. (David Beddall)

Delivered to London Central in February 2003 was MAL52 (BD52 LMO), part of the batch purchased for the 436. It shows off the length and the three-door layout of the Citaro Gs operated in London. Vauxhall Bus Station provides the backdrop to the photograph. (David Beddall)

First London took stock of thirty-two Citaro Gs in the autumn of 2003 to convert route 18 (Sudbury–Euston) to the type. This batch is represented by 11021 (LK53 FBY) seen parked at the former west London garage at Hayes. First went on to purchase a further twenty-seven of the type to convert route 207 in 2005. (Liam Farrer-Beddall)

Above and below: The 453 (Deptford Bridge–Marylebone) was the only bendy-bus route to receive two batches of Citaros. Stagecoach London took stock of thirty-five Citaros in 2003 to operate the route. The contract was lost to London General in February 2008. Above we see 23009 (LX03 HCH) at the Marylebone terminus. Below MAL97 (BD57 WDA) represents the London General fleet. The front style changed slightly between the batches as can be seen. (David Beddall)

Various road closures in central London often cause diversions to bus routes. This is the case here where East London's 23057 (LX04 LBL) is seen on diversion through London Bridge on its way to Oxford Circus. The 25s normal line of route runs from Ilford, through Stratford to its central London terminus via Holborn. The 25 was converted to bendy-bus operation in June 2004, operated by no less than forty-one Citaro Gs. (Liam Farrer-Beddall)

Arriva London converted four high-profile central London routes to bendy-bus operation in 2004 and 2005, these being the 29, 73, 38 and 149. Oxford Street finds MA65 (BX04 NCU) heading to Victoria Station on route 73. For this route, forty-seven Mercedes-Benz Citaro Gs were taken into stock by Arriva London. The route was reallocated to Lea Valley garage from Tottenham, as the latter did not have the space to accommodate the large fleet. (Liam Farrer-Beddall)

Route 38 was the penultimate London service to be converted to bendy-bus operation, when on 29 October 2005 fifty-eight Citaros replaced Routemasters on this service. MA116 (BX55 FVS) is seen loading at Hackney Central, operating a short working to Hyde Park Corner. (David Beddall)

Two years after the Volvo B7TL model was introduced to the streets of London, examples were purchased by London General of the East Lancs Myllennium model. Fifty-two such vehicles were taken into stock at Sutton garage to convert a number of double-deck routes from that garage. The type operated with the company for around seven years before being replaced by the Optare Olympus-bodied ADL Trident DOE-class. EVL42 (PJ02 PYZ) is seen parked at the side of Sutton bus garage. (David Beddall)

Fifty-five of the East Lancs Myllennium-bodied Volvo B7TL double-deck model was taken into stock by London United. Ten were shorter than the majority, taking up the class code VE. The VLE, as seen above, was the standard length. VLE6 (PG04 WHJ) was one of a number allocated to Stamford Brook garage for route 9 (Aldwych–Hammersmith). (Liam Farrer-Beddall)

Durham Travel Services (DTS) won the contract for the 42 (Denmark Hill–Liverpool Street) and commenced operation on this route in April 2002. For this service, the company, trading as Easylink, chose the East Lancs Myllennium-bodied Scania N94UB OmniCity, the only examples of this type in London service. The first examples entered the fleet in July 2002, slightly later than planned. In August 2002, DTS went into liquidation, with the route and vehicles passing to East Thames Buses. Liverpool Street finds SE08 (YU02 GHK) showing route branding for the 42. (Ian Armstrong Collection)

Metrobus was the only TfL operator to take stock of the Scania OmniCity single-decker. The company purchased seventy examples for operation both on London services and for the company's West Sussex operations. Seventeen arrived with the company in November 2003 to operate route 358 (Crystal Palace–Orpington Station). Above we see 522 (YN53 RXP) loading having just left the Crystal Palace terminus. (Liam Farrer-Beddall)

CT Plus introduced the East Lancs Myllennium to London in January 2003, when thirteen such vehicles arrived on Trident chassis. They were put to use on the 388 (Blackfriars–Hackney Wick) and remain as the only examples of this type to have operated in the capital. The rebuilding of Blackfriars Station, which commenced in 2008, saw the route extended to Temple, with buses running in service down Victoria Embankment. It is this location where we find HTL3 (LR52 LTJ). (Liam Farrer-Beddall)

Transdev London placed a sizable order for the Scania N94UD model, with sixty-four such vehicles entering the London United and London Sovereign fleets in 2004 and 2005. The London Sovereign division took stock of the type primarily to operate route 13 (Aldwych–Golders Green), replacing AEC Routemasters. SLE23 (YN55 NHV) is seen passing through Piccadilly Circus, completing the last leg of its journey from Golders Green. (David Beddall)

The dominant low-floor double-deck choice for Metrobus was the Scania N94UD Omnidekka, of which the company purchased 116. Eleven of the type arrived with the company in March 2006 to operate route 127 (Tooting Broadway–Purley). 920 (YN06 JYE) represents this batch, and is seen on layover at the Tooting Broadway terminus. (Liam Farrer-Beddall)

After serving the capital in mainstream service, a number of former London buses are retained by their owners and used in a variety of ways. Go-Ahead London kept former Metrobus 935 (YN56 FDK) and placed it into their commercial services fleet. It is seen on layover at Old Steine, Brighton, having completed a seasonal service in from the capital. Note the gold fleet names and white band in between decks, which makes these vehicles stand out from the typical TfL buses. (Liam Farrer-Beddall).

East Thames Buses established a garage in Belvedere, south-east London. From here a number of routes were operated including the 108 (Lewisham–Stratford). Twenty-five SB120 saloons were ordered against the tender win for this route. The company acquired these vehicles through Volvo, who called them the Volvo Merit. There were a generous number of spare vehicles from the 108, which had a PVR of eighteen. This led to the type appearing on other routes. This is shown above, DWL33 (FJ54 ZDC) is seen on layover in Bexleyheath town centre while operating route 132 (Eltham Station–Bexleyheath). (David Beddall)

Another variation of the Gemini model was the Pulsar, which was available on the DAF and VDL DB250 chassis. The Arriva operations in London were the only recipients of this model. Arriva London South took stock of a large quantity of the type to operate routes in the Croydon area. DW9 (LJ03 MVW) is seen passing through Croydon, displaying the so-called 'Cow Horn' livery. (Liam Farrer-Beddall)

Arriva The Shires & Essex also took stock of a handful of the Wright Eclipse Pulsar for route 258 (South Harrow–Watford Junction). 6036 (YJ55 WOX) is seen passing Harrow Bus Station on its way to nearby South Harrow. (Liam Farrer-Beddall)

Since its introduction in December 2005, the Enviro400 has become the popular choice for many London operators. The first Enviro400 arrived with Stagecoach London during this month, numbered 18500. However, Metroline took stock of the first production batch to convert route 24. Since then, Stagecoach, First, Metroline, Go-Ahead, London United and Arriva have all taken large quantities of the Enviro400. Representing the 'Classic' Enviro400 is Stagecoach London's 10140 (LX12 DFV). It is seen passing through Bromley town centre bound for Lewisham Station on route 208. (Liam Farrer-Beddall)

The first Wrightbus ElectroCity was delivered to Go-Ahead London in December 2005, with more following during the early part of 2006. In November 2007, Travel London took stock of five ElectroCitys for short route 129 (Greenwich–North Greenwich). Unlike those delivered to Go-Ahead London, this model took parts from the newer VDL SB180 saloon. These vehicles were allocated to Walworth garage, passing to Abellio London in October 2009. June 2011 saw the loss of the 129 to Go-Ahead, with the ElectroCitys initially going into storage before being put to use from Fulwell garage in the Richmond area. They were eventually withdrawn from service at the end of 2012. 8805 (LJ57 YBB) is seen here showing off the green leaf livery worn by the initial hybrid vehicles in London. (Ian Armstrong Collection)

Metrobus seemed to favour Scania vehicles over the more conventional low-floor buses operated by other London operators. Over the course of 2006, the company took stock of twenty-three shorter Scania OmniTowns, bodied by East Lancs on the Esteem model. They were all allocated to Green Street Green garage from where they operated routes 181 and 284, centred on Lewisham. 605 (YM55 SWY) is seen approaching the now vanished Lewisham Bus Station. (Liam Farrer-Beddall)

Fifteen Scania N94UD OmniCitys were delivered to London United over the course of September and October 2006. These were the first of a large number of the OmniCity model purchased by this operator, totalling over 200 of the N94UD and N230UD variants. SP4 (YN56 FCE) is seen departing Cromwell Road Bus Station, Kingston. (Liam Farrer-Beddall)

Twenty-two further Scania N94UDs were delivered to London United during 2008. SP24 (YN08 DHK) represents the batch. Originally intended for the 482, it later transferred to Hounslow for use there. It is captured on camera just before entering Heathrow Central. March 2016 saw a renumbering of the RATP London fleet, with SP24 becoming SP40024, the number that it is seen carrying. (Liam Farrer-Beddall)

Docklands Buses were the only recipients of the MCV Evolution-bodied ADL Dart combination in London. The first of these arrived during August 2006, with more arriving in December for route W19 between Ilford and Walthamstow. Hainault Street, Ilford finds ED11 (AE56 OUK). The ED-class later passed to Go-Ahead London. (Liam Farrer-Beddall)

The East Lancs Esteem-bodied ADL Dart saloon first entered London service in 2006. Metrobus took stock of the first of the type for operation in the Croydon area. West Croydon Bus Station finds 261 (PN06 UYR). (Liam Farrer-Beddall)

CT Plus took stock of six East Lancs Esteem-bodied ADL Darts for route W13. The first of the batch, DE1 (PN07 KPY), is seen in Leytonstone. CT Plus is the name used by the Hackney Community Transport group for its TfL routes. (Liam Farrer-Beddall)

2007 saw the arrival of the first Scania N230UD fitted with an East Lancs Olympus body in London. Nine of these vehicles arrived with London United at Shepherds Bush garage in June and were put to use on the 148 (Shepherds Bush–Camberwell Green). These nine were disliked and lasted just over two years with the company. The last of batch, SO9 (YN07 LHZ) is seen parked at Shepherds Bush garage. (David Beddall)

Further examples of the Scania N230UD/East Lancs Olympus combination were taken into stock by Metroline in the summer of 2007. Twenty-two arrived to take up service on route 7 (East Acton–Russel Square). SEL744 (LK07 BAO) is seen passing through Marble Arch heading towards East Acton. The upgrade of this route led to the Scanias being pushed out to the west London suburbs. (Liam Farrer-Beddall)

The Enviro200 was first introduced in 2004, but at this time proved unpopular with operators. It wasn't until its relaunch in 2006 that it became popular, not only in London, but around the country. It eventually replaced the numerous Dennis Dart SLF saloons in service around London. First London initially took a batch into stock for route 165, operating in the Romford area. It is this location we find DML44006 (LK57 EJL). (Liam Farrer-Beddall)

As with its predecessor, the Enviro200 could be found in most of the suburbs of Greater London, as well as on a handful of routes in central London. DE30003 (YX58 DVC), originally numbered DE3 with London United, is seen exiting Brent Cross Bus Station, heading toward the edge of London, Barnet. By this time, the vehicle had transferred across to fellow RATP Group company London Sovereign. (Liam Farrer-Beddall)

Metroline took stock of thirty-eight MCV Evolution-bodied MAN 12.240 saloons during 2007. Twenty of them were used on route 232 (St Raphael's–Turnpike Lane). These were the only vehicles of this combination to operate in the capital. MM776 (LK07 AYG) is seen exiting Brent Cross Bus Station heading to St Raphael's. (Liam Farrer-Beddall)

The East London Bus Group was another fan of the Scania OmniCity, taking 174 into stock between 2008 and 2010. The first sixteen arrived over the autumn of 2008, allocated to Rainham garage for route 248 (Romford Market–Cranham). The late delivery of the batch led to the loan of Dennis Tridents to East London. In 2010 Stagecoach reacquired the East London and Selkent operations, and it is with this operator we see 15001 (LX58 CDV) passing through Romford Station. (Liam Farrer-Beddall)

Selkent's Plumstead garage took stock of a large number of the Scania OmniCity for routes 51 (Woolwich–Orpington), 53 (Plumstead Bus Garage–Whitehall) and 96 (Woolwich–Bluewater) during 2009. 15052 (LX09 ACF) shows off the Selkent fleet name applied to vehicles allocated to Plumstead garage under the ownership of the East London Bus Group. It is seen loading at Woolwich town centre, on what is now a pedestrianised area. (David Beddall)

Leyton garage took stock of the last fifty Scania OmniCitys for routes 48 (London Bridge–Walthamstow) and 56 (Leyton, Bakers Arms–St Bartholomew's Hospital). Representing the allocation is 15131 (LX59 CMK), passing through Hackney town centre, another road that buses no longer travel down. (Liam Farrer-Beddall)

CT Plus purchased ten Scania OmniCity's for use on the 212 (St James Street–Chingford Station), which were delivered in February 2010. SD7 (YR59 NPN) is seen waiting to exit Walthamstow Central Bus Station, to complete the last, small section of the route. (Liam Farrer-Beddall)

The London Sovereign operation of Transdev London received twenty of the revised Scania N230UD OmniCity model for route 183. When compared with the N94UD there is very little difference in appearance. SP40075 (YT59 RXZ), originally SP75, represents the batch. It is seen on layover in Pinner town centre. (Liam Farrer-Beddall)

The London United/London Sovereign Scania OmniCitys totalled 206 examples, delivered between 2006 and 2010. The final sixteen were purchased to operate route H91 (Hammersmith–Hounslow West). SP40204 (SP204–YR10 FGN) is seen having just departed Hammersmith Bus Station, bound for Hounslow West. (Liam Farrer-Beddall)

Two years passed before a hybrid version of the Enviro400 was introduced to London service, known as the Enviro400H. Again, like its diesel counterpart, the hybrid version was taken into stock by Stagecoach, First, Metroline and London United. The vehicles had a 'hybrid' logo applied to the side of the vehicle. London United took stock of a batch for route 94 (Acton Green–Piccadilly Circus). ADH7 (SN60 BYB) is seen on layover, with the Theatre Royal, Haymarket seen in the background. (Liam Farrer-Beddall)

Seven Polish-built Scania OmniCity saloons were taken into stock during August 2008 for use on route 293 between Morden and Epsom Hospital. Morden Station finds 561 (YN08 OAS) having just completed a journey in from Epsom. (Liam Farrer-Beddall)

Further examples of the Olympus model, this time built under the Optare name, entered London service in early 2009. Go-Ahead London took stock of fifty-four double-decks based on the ADL Trident chassis, classifying them DOE. Representing the batch is DOE10 (LX58 CWZ), seen passing through Croydon heading for Morden on route 154. All but one of this class were originally allocated to Sutton garage. (Liam Farrer-Beddall)

The first Optare Tempos arrived in London in December 2008 with the East London Bus Group. Ten hybrid Tempos were split between East London and Metroline, with the remainder arriving in London during 2009. 25111 (YJ08 PGO) was new to East London for the 276 (Stoke Newington–Newham General Hospital) but transferred within the group to Selkent at Plumstead for use on route 380 (Belmarsh–Lewisham) in 2011. 25111 was new to the company as 29001 and is seen passing through Lewisham bound for Belmarsh. (Liam Farrer-Beddall)

The five Tempos with Metroline entered service from Brentford garage on route E8, operating alongside standard Enviro200 saloons. OTH972 (LK58 CTZ) was delivered to Metroline in February 2009. Photographed at Ealing Broadway, OTH972 shows off the green leaf livery that was applied to the ten hybrid Tempos. (David Beddall)

2009 saw the introduction of the Optare Versa to London service. London United took delivery of the first batch in January. The contract renewal on route 391, in December 2008, saw London United purchase nineteen Optare Versas. The penultimate one of the batch, OV18 (YJ58 VBY), is seen departing Hammersmith Bus Station for Richmond. (Liam Farrer-Beddall)

Two batches of Optare Versas were taken into stock by the East London Bus Group in 2009. The first nine were allocated to the Selkent division for route 469 (Bexleyheath–Queen Elizabeth Hospital). Numerically the first example in the fleet was 37001 (LX58 CHF), seen passing Woolwich Arsenal Docklands Light Railway station in Woolwich town centre. This batch of nine were delivered in February 2009 and shows the Selkent logos. (David Beddall)

OVL56 (YJ09 EYT) formed part of a batch of seventeen Optare Versa saloons taken into stock by NCP Challenger in February and March 2009 for route 283 (Hammersmith–Barnes). The majority of the batch was late arriving, including this example, which led to the hire of a number of Dennis Dart SLFs from London United. The lower bus station at Hammersmith provides the location of this photograph. (David Beddall)

Epsom Buses (Quality Line) took stock of the Optare Versa in September 2010 for the take up of route 411 (Kingston–West Molesey) in September 2010. OV07 (YJ60 KGO) is seen departing Cromwell Road Bus Station, Kingston, showing off the dual-door layout of these vehicles. (Liam Farrer-Beddall)

Optare Limited loaned a hybrid Optare Versa to London between 2011 and 2018. OP07 ARE originally operated with London Central on route 360 from Camberwell from September 2011. It moved on to Epsom Buses (Quality Line) in November 2015. It is seen passing through Kingston town centre. Note the dome at the rear of the vehicle, making it stand out from other Versas operating in London. (Liam Farrer-Beddall)

Three ADL Enviro400-bodied Volvo B9TLs were taken into stock by Go-Ahead London in October 2008. These remain the only three of this type to operate in the UK. VE2 (LX58 CWL) is seen about to pass Cromwell Road Bus Station, Kingston, while heading back to its home garage of Sutton. (Liam Farrer-Beddall)

Go-Ahead London took stock of the ADL Dart saloon in 2009 for routes 163 and 164. By 2009 East Lancs had been purchased by Optare, and the Esteem model renamed simply as the 'Optare Esteem'. SOE3 (LX09 AYH) shows off its Optare badge while on layover in Wimbledon town centre. (Liam Farrer-Beddall)

SOE13 (LX09 AYU) is another example of the Optare Esteem. Morden Underground Station provides the backdrop to this photograph. SOE13 was allocated to London General's Merton garage. (Liam Farrer-Beddall)

2009 saw the introduction of an integral double-deck model from Wrightbus. Chassis components for the model were sourced from VDL, and subsequently it was dubbed the VDL DB300/Wrightbus Gemini 2 model. Arriva London took large numbers of this type between 2009 and 2012. Upon the conversion of route 38 from bendy-bus to double-deck operation, a large quantity of the type was taken into stock by Arriva. The first of this batch was numbered DW201 (LJ09 KRO), which is seen operating from Grays garage on route 103, paused at Romford Station. (Liam Farrer-Beddall)

DW411 (LJ11 AEB) is another fine example of the DB300/Gemini 2 combination, representing the 2011 delivery. It is seen operating from Ponders End garage, about to enter Edmonton Green Bus Station on a working of route 349 to its home garage. (Liam Farrer-Beddall)

East Lancs went into administration in 2007, the company being purchased by the Darwen Group. It is this company who purchased Optare in June 2008. By this time the East Lancs and Darwen names were dropped in favour of the Optare name. Therefore, the Olympus model became known as the Optare Olympus. Metrobus took stock of thirty examples of this type on the Scania N230UD chassis in 2009 for routes 54 and 75. 887 (PN09 ENE) is seen here almost at journey's end in Woolwich. (Liam Farrer-Beddall)

Metrobus was the only London company to take stock of a batch of MCV Evolution-bodied MAN 14.240 single-decks. Fifteen such vehicles arrived with the company between February and April 2009, entering service on route 202 (Crystal Palace–Blackheath). 714 (AJ58 WBE) is photographed at Crystal Palace. (Liam Farrer-Beddall)

The Volvo B5LH hybrid double-deck chassis entered service in London during the summer of 2009, with five of these vehicles being taken into stock by Arriva London in June 2009 carrying the original Gemini body style. The trial of these vehicles was successful, which led to further orders for the type by Arriva. HV2 (LJ09 KOE) is seen rounding Elephant & Castle after undergoing a repaint and refurbishment. It is seen sporting the new Arriva logos. (Liam Farrer-Beddall)

After the success of the Eclipse Gemini, Wrightbus redeveloped the model to become the Gemini 2. There was a gap of around three years between the end of production of the first Gemini and the introduction of the Gemini 2. Go-Ahead London, First and Metroline took a number of the type on the Volvo B9TL chassis, favouring this combination over the Enviro400. 291 were purchased by First London between 2009 and 2012. VN37830 (BG59 FXD) shows off the type while exiting Walthamstow Bus Station. (Liam Farrer-Beddall)

Metroline first took stock of Eclipse Gemini 2-bodied B9TL model in 2010 for use on its route 237 (White City–Hounslow Heath). Shepherds Bush station finds VW1035 (LK10 BXC), almost at journey's end. A difference in the Gemini 2 bodywork of the B9TL and B5LH can be seen when compared with a photograph of VWH1362 later in this book. (Liam Farrer-Beddall)

Like its predecessor, the B7TL, the Volvo B9TL proved to be a popular model with the Go-Ahead London group. WVL376 (LX60 DXG) was allocated to London Central, operating from its Bexleyheath garage. It is seen at Woolwich, heading back to Bexleyheath on route 422. (Liam Farrer-Beddall)

A second attempt at operating hydrogen fuel cell buses commenced in 2011 with six Wright Pulsar-bodied VDL SB200 saloons, the first of which was delivered during November 2010. central London route RV1 was again the route chosen for the trial. Three additional vehicles of the same type were delivered to First London between 2011 and 2013. WSH62992 (LK60 HPF) shows off the type, rounding the Imax cinema at Waterloo. The branding applied to the vehicles can be clearly seen in this view. (Liam Farrer-Beddall)

Both Metroline and Go-Ahead London also took stock of a number of Volvo B5LHs. VWH1362 (LK62 DJY) was one of five such vehicles taken into stock by Metroline for route 24. They worked alongside diesel Wright Eclipse Gemini 2-bodied Volvo B9TLs on the route. VWH1362 is seen rounding Trafalgar Square, heading north to Hampstead Heath. (Liam Farrer-Beddall)

By the time the next batch of B5LHs arrived with Arriva London, Wrightbus had produced the new Gemini 2 model, with a revised front styling. The Gemini 2 became a popular body on both the B5LH and B9TL chassis with a number of London operators. HV67 (LJ62 BND) represents the type and is seen at London Bridge before travelling back to Palmers Green on route 141. (Liam Farrer-Beddall)

Two years passed before any further Optare Tempos entered service in London. Sixteen diesel-powered Tempos were purchased by London United for use on route H37 (Hounslow, Blenheim Centre–Richmond), displacing Dennis Dart SLF saloons. All examples were allocated to Hounslow garage, and arrived between March and May 2011. OT2 (YJ11 EHH) is seen loading in Hounslow town centre nearing journey's end. (Liam Farrer-Beddall)

The first MCV double-decker arrived in London in May 2011 when Go-Ahead London's Docklands Buses subsidiary took stock of a solitary example on the Volvo B9TL chassis. It was trialled on routes from Silvertown garage. VM1 (BJ11 XGZ) is seen attending the Showbus 2011 rally at the Imperial War Museum, Duxford. Tour operator Golden Tours was the only other operator in London to take stock of this type. MCV would later produce the more successful EvoSeti model. (Liam Farrer-Beddall)

A rival to the Optare Solo was introduced by Wrightbus, Ballymena, in 2010. Known as the Streetlite, it came in three forms; the wheel forward (WF), door forward (DF) and Max, the latter two being longer the WF model being shorter. The first Streetlites to enter service in London came in the form of the WF model. Go-Ahead London's Blue Triangle subsidiary was the first to take stock of the type. WS1 (LJ12 CGF) formed part of a batch of nine delivered in March 2012 for route 462 (Ilford–Hainault). WS1 is photographed passing through Ilford Broadway. The loss of route 462 to Stagecoach London saw the Streetlites transfer to Orpington for use on local services in that area. (Liam Farrer-Beddall)

Go-Ahead London was the only operator to take stock of the Streetlite WF from new. 2017 saw ten WFs enter service from Putney garage on route 424 (Putney Heath–Fulham), displacing shorter Plaxton Pointer-bodied Dennis Dart SLF saloons. WS82 (SK17 HKB) is seen travelling down Putney High Street. (Liam Farrer-Beddall)

Quality Line purchased several Streetlite WFs from Wrightbus that had formerly operated with Go-Ahead London. WS20265 (SN64 CUA) was used on route 463 (Coulsdon South–Pollards Hill), replacing Optare Solos on the route in 2016. It is seen passing through Coulsdon town centre. (Liam Farrer-Beddall)

The first bus specifically designed for London since the AEC Routemaster back in 1954 was placed into service during 2012. Eight prototypes of the Wrightbus New Bus for London (NBfL) 'Borrismaster' were delivered between March and July of this year and put to use on the 38 (Clapton Pond–Victoria). LT6 (LT12 FHT) is seen passing Green Park, with The Ritz hotel in the background. This vehicle was later reregistered LTZ 1006, the LTZ registration marks being reserved for this type. (Liam Farrer-Beddall)

The NBfL was changed to the New Routemaster from LT513 onwards, with no difference at all between them. The LT-class were unique vehicles in many ways. They were the only double-decks to operate in London with three doors and two staircases. The three-door layout can be seen clearly on LT621 (LTZ 1621), seen operating with Abellio London on route 159 at Parliament Square. (Liam Farrer-Beddall)

ST812 (LTZ 1812) is the shortest of the New Routemasters, measuring a metre shorter than the LT class. It was constructed this way to compensate for an issue with the turning circle at the Crouch End Broadway terminus of route 91. However, this was rectified, and no further vehicles of this length were built, making ST812 unique. It is seen blinded for the annual Imberbus running day across Salisbury Plain. St Pancras International provides the backdrop for this photograph. (Liam Farrer-Beddall)

November 2012 saw the arrival of eight Optare Solo SR saloons at Quality Line for route 470 between Colliers Wood and Epsom. Built to dual-door layout, these were the first examples of the SR model to enter service on London contracts. OPL07 (YJ62 FXG) is seen completing the last leg of its journey to Colliers Wood at Sutton town centre. (Liam Farrer-Beddall)

Routes H2 and H3 transferred to the control of Metroline at Cricklewood garage in June 2018. For this, a similar number of Optare Solo SR saloons were ordered, and as can be seen above, were very short. However, they were late in arriving, so the former Arriva Solos were placed on loan to Metroline until the arrival of the new vehicles. OS 2503 (YJ68 FXE) is seen at Golders Green sporting its new electronic white destination display. (Liam Farrer-Beddall)

Go-Ahead London was again first to introduce the Wrightbus Streetlite DF model. Eleven such vehicles were purchased in May and June 2013 for route 219 (Wimbledon–Clapham Junction). WS18 (LJ13 GKE) is seen representing the batch on route 219. The DF model became more popular with London operators, with the type being available in varying lengths. (Liam Farrer-Beddall)

Arriva London took stock of the Streetlite DF model in October 2016, with a second batch arriving in the summer of 2017. From the second batch is SLS29 (SK17 HJW), seen passing East Croydon Station bound for Crystal Palace on route 410. This is a shorter model than WS13 seen previously. (Liam Farrer-Beddall)

2017 also saw the arrival of twenty DF saloons with Tower Transit at Lea Interchange garage for route 236 (Hackney Wick–Finsbury Park). WV46214 (SK17 HGP) represents the batch while passing Homerton Hospital, Hackney. (Liam Farrer-Beddall)

Go-Ahead London began the search for a more environmentally friendly single-deck type to operate its central London routes 507 and 521 in 2013, using a pair of all-electric BYD K9E saloons. Transport for London was keen to promote this new technology, and the green leaf livery applied to the first hybrid vehicles back in 2008 was again applied to these vehicles. These BYDs were taken into stock to see how successful they would be on the 507 and 521, operating from Go-Ahead London's Waterloo garage. EB2 (LC63 CXY) is seen on layover at Waterloo Station before heading back to Victoria on route 507. (Liam Farrer-Beddall)

A more unusual buy by the Stagecoach Group were thirty-two Wright Eclipse Gemini 3-bodied Volvo B5LH double-decks, a new type introduced to London in 2014. 13001–32 entered service on route 53 (Whitehall–Plumstead), naturally being allocated to Selkents Plumstead garage. 13003 (BU14 EFY) is seen at Parliament Square about to travel up Whitehall to its terminus near Horse Guards Parade. The batch was withdrawn in 2019, passing to Arriva London, who classified them 'HV'. (Liam Farrer-Beddall)

London United also took stock of a number of the Gemini 3-bodied Volvo B5LH, putting them into service on route 285 (Heathrow Central–Kingston). VH29 (LJ15 JZE) is seen at Heathrow Airport shortly before entering the central area of the airport. (Liam Farrer-Beddall)

In 2015 the Gemini underwent yet another restyling, giving the Gemini 3 the appearance of a Wrightbus Streetdeck. Go-Ahead London was the first to take stock of the type for its Metrobus operations in south-east London, converting routes 119 and 202. Crystal Palace finds WHV69 (BF65 WJU) showing off the new body style. (Liam Farrer-Beddall)

Metroline took stock of over 250 Wright Eclipse Gemini 3-bodied Volvo B5LH double-decks to replace a large number of Plaxton President double-decks in the fleet. VWH2185 (LK16 HZC) is seen on layover at Ruislip Station blinded for its return journey to Mill Hill Broadway. (Liam Farrer-Beddall)

The Optare MetroCity was first introduced to London in October 2014 when a pair were delivered to Arriva London's Croydon garage. The conversion of route 312 (South Croydon–Norwood Junction) in September led to further deliveries of the type. EMC2 (LK64 DWJ) was one of the original pair and is seen passing through Croydon town centre, nearing journey's end. The green leaf livery was applied to this batch of vehicles, having disappeared from London's buses after the initial hybrid vehicles appeared in London in 2008. The tag line 'I am an electric bus' can be seen on the side of the vehicle. (Liam Farrer-Beddall)

The AD E40H/Enviro400 MMC model was a more popular choice with London operators compared to the diesel variant, and was introduced in 2015. The first of the type were delivered to Abellio London in December 2014. London Sovereign's ADH45278 (YX68 UNH) represents the numerous examples of the type to operate in the capital. It is seen heading through a wet Pinner town centre, bound for South Harrow. (Liam Farrer-Beddall)

Go-Ahead London was by far the biggest customer of the AD E40H/Enviro400 MMC model, taking in excess of 250 of the type into stock. EH126 (SN66 WOY) is photographed at Bishopsgate, close to Liverpool Street Station, operating a journey on route 42. (Liam Farrer-Beddall)

The 2015 vehicle order for the Stagecoach Group included forty-two AD Enviro400 MMCs fitted to the Volvo B5LH chassis for its London operations. The first twenty-one were allocated to Plumstead garage for route 122. 13065 (BF15 KGV) represents the batch while heading to Thamesmead, while passing through Woolwich town centre. (Liam Farrer-Beddall)

The remaining twenty-one Volvo B5LHs were allocated to Catford garage for route 47 (Bellingham–Shoreditch). However, they were also used on the garage's other double-deck routes from time to time as illustrated by 13102 (BL65 OYY), which is seen in Lewisham heading for Catford garage (Bellingham), on route 199. (Liam Farrer-Beddall)

Stagecoach London was the first operator to take stock of the diesel version of the AD E40D model, complete with the new Enviro400 MMC body style. 10301 (WLT 546, originally YY15 OYS) is numerically the first of the type. It is seen passing under the rail bridges at Romford Station. It gained its green-based livery for MacMillan Cancer Support in June 2018. (Liam Farrer-Beddall)

In June 2015, a pair of all-electric Irizar i2 saloons were taken into stock to operate alongside a pair of BYD K9E all-electric saloons operating on routes 507 and 521. They wore the green leaf livery, and carried branding promoting the all-electric credentials. EI1 (YP15 NLM) is seen showing off this livery while loading at Tenyson Way, Waterloo, before setting off for London Bridge. (Liam Farrer-Beddall)

October 2017 saw the arrival of another Irizar i2 electric bus, this time allocated to CT Plus, similar to the pair taken into stock by Go-Ahead London on the 507 and 521 services. The vehicle was registered YN67 VDK and is seen departing Finsbury Park Bus Station out of service. (Liam Farrer-Beddall)

Go-Ahead London's Docklands Buses subsidiary took stock of sixteen AD Enviro400 MMC-bodied Volvo B5TL diesel double-decks in June 2015 for operation on route 135. EHV9 (BL15 HBU) is seen at Bishopsgate heading for Crossharbour. A Scania OmniCity of Stagecoach London can be glimpsed next to EHV9, operating route 48 to London Bridge. (Liam Farrer-Beddall)

In 2014, ADL relaunched its Enviro range as the MMC (Major Model Change). After this date, the Enviro models referred to previously in this book were referred to as the 'classic'. Like the other Enviro200s, the MMC version became popular again with operators. ENN39 (YY67 HCA) is seen passing Wood Green Underground Station showing off the type well. (Liam Farrer-Beddall)

With the exception of Tower Transit, all other London operators took stock of the Enviro200 MMC saloon. The RATP Group took a large number for contract gains in North London. Route 288 was won from Arriva London in 2018 and restocked with the type. DLE30259 (SK68 TLU) is seen changing drivers at Edgware Bus Station. (Liam Farrer-Beddall)

ADL was the first to introduce the electric double-decker to the streets of London in October 2015. Three 'virtual electric' Enviro400 MMCs were placed into service with Tower Transit on route 69 (Walthamstow–Canning Town), mainly operating in electric mode, as promoted on this side. The last of the trio, DH38503 (SN65 ZGR) is photographed exiting Walthamstow Bus Station. Having been delivered to Tower Transit in November 2015, it is seen wearing the green leaf livery. (Liam Farrer-Beddall)

2015 saw the introduction of another variant of the Enviro400 range, the Enviro400 City. Originally available on the AD E40H chassis, it was later offered on a Scania chassis in the provinces, and in 2019 on the BYD chassis. Arriva London took stock of the first examples of the type for route 78 (Nunhead–Shoreditch). Showing off the smart design is HA10 (LK65 BZG), seen passing through Peckham. (Liam Farrer-Beddall)

CT Plus was the only other operator to take stock of the AD E40H/Enviro400 City combination. The company won route 26 from Tower Transit in 2016. 2516 (SN16 OJF) is seen leaving Waterloo for Hackney Wick. The upgrade of route 388, and the gain of route 20 in north-west London saw further Enviro400 Citys enter service with the company. (Liam Farrer-Beddall)

Chinese-built BYD became the forerunner in the all-electric bus market, with a large quantity of its products entering service in London from 2016. Five BYD K8SR models were taken into stock by Transport for London and allocated to Metroline for trials. Based at the company's Willesden garage, the quintet could be found operating route 98. The trial ended in November 2019, with the vehicles being withdrawn from service. Marble Arch finds BYD1474 (LJ16 EZP), heading back to its home garage sporting the green leaf livery. (Liam Farrer-Beddall)

2016 saw the release of the newer MCV EvoSeti model based on the Volvo B5LH chassis. This proved to be much more popular with London operators than the original MCV double-deck body released in 2011. Go-Ahead London was the first customer of the type, with eighty-five being taken into stock by Camberwell garage over the course of the year. St Pancras International provides the backdrop for MHV38 (BG66 MJF), which is seen about to head to Honor Oak on route 63. (Liam Farrer-Beddall)

Tower Transit took stock of fifty-one MCV EvoSeti-bodied Volvo B5LHs for routes 13 and 308. Route 13 underwent a transformation in 2017, replacing the 82. The central terminus for the route moved from Aldwych to Victoria. Hyde Park Corner finds MV38204 (LJ17 WRE) heading north to its new northern terminus of North Finchley. The more subtle hybrid logo can be seen just behind the rear wheel. (Liam Farrer-Beddall)

The road outside Homerton Hospital finds Tower Transit's MV38246 (LJ17 WTW), while operating the 308 to Wanstead. The 308 starts from near-by Clapton Pond and has the smaller PVR of the two routes. (Liam Farrer-Beddall)

Metroline became the third operator to take stock of the EvoSeti. The first routes to be converted were the 30 and 274 in central London. Next, it was the turn of the 113 (Edgware–Marble Arch). VMH was the class code allocated to the type by the company. VMH2439 (LK18 AFU) is seen about to enter Edgware Bus Station, having just completed its long journey in from central London. (Liam Farrer-Beddall)

2016 saw the introduction of the Wrightbus SRM-bodied Volvo B5LH. The SRM took features from the NBfL but featured the standard single staircase and dual-door layout. They were originally used on route 13 (Golders Green–Aldwych), but would occasionally stray onto other routes as can be seen above. Class code VHR were given to the type by London Sovereign. LJ66 EZT was numbered VHR45207 and is seen loading at Tennyson Way, Waterloo, on route 139. The loss of route 13 led to the type transferring to route 183. Just six of the type were built. (Liam Farrer-Beddall)

The first Wrightbus Streetdecks to enter service in London were in the form of two demonstrators arriving in January 2015. The first production models arrived in June 2016 for route 340 (Edgware–Harrow), with nine being delivered to Arriva The Shires, who by this time were under the control of Arriva London. These were similar in appearance to the Wright Eclipse Gemini 3. SW8 (LK16 BXL) is seen on layover at Edgware Bus Station. (Liam Farrer-Beddall)

Go-Ahead London took stock of a larger batch of eighteen Wrightbus Streetdecks in May 2018 for route 44 (Tooting Broadway–Victoria), allocated to near-by Merton garage. WSD11 SN18 XZE is seen passing through Tooting Broadway, almost at journey's end. (Liam Farrer-Beddall)

The first production batch of all-electric single-decks to operate in London were constructed by BYD. The first fifty-one were purchased by Go-Ahead London for central London routes 507 and 521. SEe14 (LJ66 CFN) is seen rounding the Imax Cinema at Waterloo, having just completed a journey from London Bridge. The bodywork is built by ADL, with the Enviro200EV MMC model. This batch are longer than others operated by Go-Ahead and is known as the D9UR model. (Liam Farrer-Beddall)

A third type of hydrogen-powered single-deck bus was placed into service in London in 2017. Again, the RV1 was the route chosen for this trial. A pair of Van Hool A330FC saloons arrived in August 2017 at Tower Transit's Lea Interchange garage, wearing full green-leaf livery. BH63101 (LJ67 HTF) represents the batch and is seen about to enter the Aldwych, having just crossed Waterloo Bridge. After the withdrawal of the RV1, these vehicles along with the SB200s were put to use on the 444 (Chingford–Turnpike Lane). (Liam Farrer-Beddall)

A slightly different order was for the Mercedes-Benz Citaro K model, of which nine were ordered by Epsom Buses for route 413. MCS09 (BV66 GYG) is seen passing through Sutton en route for Morden, being delivered to the company in November 2016. Other than a demonstrator numbered MBK1, these are currently the only Citaro Ks in operation in London. (Liam Farrer-Beddall)

LJ16 EZS is an example of the BYD K8UR model. The bus is an all-electric, and appropriate branding was applied to the vehicle. It is seen operating route 153 at Holloway Road, operating the route alongside the newly introduced BYD D8UR SEe class saloons. It was numbered EB3 for the duration of its stay with the company. (Liam Farrer-Beddall)

Twenty-three BYD D8URs were taken into stock by Metroline over the summer of 2018 for the upgrade of route 46 from standard Enviro200s. BEL2519 (LJ18 FHS) is seen heading for Bart's Hospital at the side of St Pancras International. (Liam Farrer-Beddall)

Go-Ahead London also took stock of the BYD D8UR model, these being shorter than the first SEe-class saloons purchased by the company. SEe68 (LJ67 DKU) was one of eleven such vehicles taken into stock for route 153 (Finsbury Park–Moorgate). It is seen passing through Holloway Road. (Liam Farrer-Beddall)

London United also took stock of the BYD D8UR saloon for routes 70 and C1. The London United BYDs were classified BE. Ladbrooke Grove Sainsburys finds BE37014 (LJ18 FJV), heading towards Chiswick. (Liam Farrer-Beddall)

Another all-electric single-deck to be trialled in London was the Yutong Pelican. YG18 CVS was numbered YT1 while in London service. It was placed on loan to numerous London operators for just over a year. Photographed at Mile End while under control of Stagecoach London, it is blinded for the return journey on route 323 to Canning Town. (Liam Farrer-Beddall)

A more unusual type to enter trials in London during 2018 was a BCI FBC6123BRZ5 tri-axle double-deck. The vehicle was sourced through Ensignbus, Purfleet, who operate a number of two-axle and tri-axle versions of the BCI. Numbered TA1 (LX18 DGF), it was allocated to Go-Ahead London's Camberwell garage where it was trialled on route 12. TA1 is captured at Parliament Square having just crossed Westminster Bridge. (Liam Farrer-Beddall)

A modified version of the AD E40H was introduced in 2018, known as the AD E40D 'Smart Hybrid'. Stagecoach London took a large number of the type, allocating them to garages both sides of the Thames. Abellio London took an initial batch of five to compliment older rolling stock on newly won route 207 (White City–Hayes By-Pass). 2001 (YX19 ORG) is seen rounding Shepherds Bush Green on its way to the latter destination. Physically the type shows no outward differences to the standard E40H model. (Liam Farrer-Beddall)

The first Wrightbus Streetdeck HEV96 model entered service with Arriva London in September 2018. The first production batch arrived in March 2019 when twenty-eight entered service with Tower Transit, this being a slightly modified version of the Streetdeck. WH31109 (SK19 FDJ) is seen passing Mile End Underground station in a thundery downpour. Based at Lea Interchange, they were put to use on the 25 (Ilford–City Thameslink). (Liam Farrer-Beddall)

The first production batch of all-electric double-decks entered service with Metroline in 2019 on route 43 (Friern Barnet–London Bridge). The chassis is built by BYD, with ADL building the bodywork. Holloway Road finds BDE2617 (LJ19 CUC) soon after delivery to Metroline. (Liam Farrer-Beddall)

Metroline's BDE2627 (LJ19 CVA) is seen here departing London Bridge Station for Friern Barnet. The body style chosen for this new double-deck model was the Enviro400 City. (Liam Farrer-Beddall)

The newest addition to the low-floor range is the Optare MetroDecker. Two prototypes were placed on loan with London operators from Optare, the first arriving in July 2016. The second arrived in November 2017 with Metroline registered YJ17 FXX but was not used by them. In December, it moved on to Go-Ahead London who numbered it MD1. As can be seen above, MD1 carried the green-leaf livery. (Liam Farrer-Beddall)

Metroline took stock of the first production batch of Optare MetroDeckers in London. Allocated to Potters Bar garage, they took up service on route 134, although they were quite slow in doing so. OME2665 (YJ19 HVT) is seen on delivery to London, passing Toddington Services in Bedfordshire, while promoting its 100 per cent electric credentials. (Liam Farrer-Beddall)